Oranges in January

Pansy Maurer-Alvarez

NEWTON-LE-WILLOWS

Published in the United Kingdom in 2016
by The Knives Forks And Spoons Press,
122 Birley Street,
Newton-le-Willows,
Merseyside,
WA12 9UN.

ISBN 978-1-909443-77-8

Copyright © Pansy Maurer-Alvarez, 2016.

The right of Pansy Maurer-Alvarez to be identified as the author of this work has been asserted by her in accordance with the Copyrights, Designs and Patents Act of 1988. All rights reserved. No part of this publication may be reproduced, stored in a retrieval system, transmitted in any form or by any means, electronic, photocopying, recording or otherwise, without prior permission of the publisher.

Acknowledgements:

I would like to express deep gratitude to Alice Notley for years of inspiration, mentoring and friendship.

I would also like to thank the editors of the following publications where some of these poems first appeared: *Burning Bush 2, Cancan, Hanging Loose Magazine, Issue ZERO, La Traductière, Liminal Pleasures, Osiris, Poems for a Liminal Age Anthology, Poetry Salzburg Review, Presa Magazine, Tears in the Fence, The Bastille, The Café Review, those that this, Upstairs at Duroc, Veer About 2010-2011* and *12X2 Poésie contemporaine des deux rives*.

– **Pansy Maurer-Alvarez**

Cover art: Collage, *Pensée*, 2008 by Alice Notley

Cover photo: Sabine Dundure Photography

TABLE OF CONTENTS

I. *In Memory of the Unclaimed*

Particular (*for stars)*	13
May, Apparently from a Calendar	14
In Memory of the Unclaimed	16
Particular (*for sunrays*)	18
Spring's Sudden This Year and Things Change	20
Coming and Going in Rain	22
Barely How the Wind Blows	23
Particular (*for clouds*)	24
Architecture	25
First Awareness of the Blue Line	28
Particular (*for snow*)	29
Things on the Floor	30
Water-meadow with Birches	32
Words Cut up and Pasted in the Margins	33
Valediction	34
Deed	35
"Without Noise or Spectacle"	36
The Glimmering Long Windows of an Afterthought	37
Wisdom, the Immigrant, Earth	40
The Beautiful Spelling of Common Words . . .	43

Archaeology of the Living Component . . .   44

"Cluttered Crystal"   45

Twigs, Bunches and Tangles   47

(A Window Flew Open)   49

II. *Januaries*

Symbols from the Father-like Dreams   53

Tangible   56

(The Curtains Opened)   57

(The Doors Swing Open)   58

In the Forecourt of Familiar Sounds   59

Carnations (I)   61

Nightfall   62

A Voyage in Yellow Light   63

Draw Me Closer   65

Carnations (II)   66

December   67

The Outer Rim   68

Still Radiant, Tranquil Spirit   70

Portraits in the House   71

What We Resemble   74

Beauteous Arbour   75

The Distance Between Our Continents   76

III. *A Dream of Deliverance*

Whatever You Wrote on My Drawing	83
Absence: a Pastoral	88
A Dream of Deliverance	89
Picture of Fictitious Watchman with Hawks	93
Restless Depiction Including a Water Angel	95
For the Centonarii	98
Performance Piece for Notebooks	102
Seven Video Clips	104
Poem	111
Interchangeable Distractions	112
When You Think You've Neared the End . . .	113
Interim	114
Scattered Beads	115
Some Rooms were Fictionally Red	117
We Fit in a Room	118

To the memory of
Myrtle Ruth Howry Funk
(1892 – 1976)

How
swiftly
the sun fell
out of the sky
of your ruby heart
burning holes in my tongue
blood churning through new pig valves
no hotter than the falling rain
your smile a surprise flower
offered to a stranger
closing down on the
transient dream
of childhood
baptised
love

– **Norrie Blaquart**

I

In Memory of the Unclaimed

Oranges in January

PARTICULAR (*for stars*)

If "this particular
emotion
is red"   because he said so
in the blue tent filled with roses

   (there was a small oriental-looking carpet in one corner
   candelabrum of metal roses and a mirror with fringe
     a few golden wall mosaics)

then the Seine will awaken in me   Tunisia.
What else he told me there didn't stick in my mind only
       the red inside that blue

   And now I wonder how far was
     that red from sun
       from blue
 in the blue tent where the man had invited me to write
       beside his mirror.

I must have seen
   kaleidoscopic movement on green
      near water
  bright ships outside us there
     beyond the white
     (pages?)

    waiting
    for the vast skyness
      of night   I must have.

Pansy Maurer-Alvarez

MAY, APPARENTLY FROM A CALENDAR
Simon Bening, late 1540s or early 1550s

May, apparently from a calendar   green
month of weddings
of trembling newborn
leaves   this allover green
Two black and white storks, one white horse
And there you are on the river with your
musicians and your friends
the drinks in a bag, cool in the river
for later
Let the red pageant
cross the bridge above you unnoticed
into the medieval
Red   that elaborate colour
with a crowd waiting
and a tight circle of children's games
another circle of soldiers
Red despite this profusion
of green   those filigree dots
to decorate your boat with
so much care

A woman wearing red is reflected in the river as she bends at the waist
to do her laundry, her hands centred in momentary circles

Light is gradual over this river
I can feel it leaving my shoulders and arms
feel it leaving rooms in the town and become
black cloth   night
midwinter night

Oranges in January

reclining against my side insistingly
Your voice inside my ear when you phoned from Sweden –
your red laser voice
high above the memory of our river
I feel you so close I can draw you there

Pansy Maurer-Alvarez

IN MEMORY OF THE UNCLAIMED

Against this strong afternoon light I remember a bird
     elongated
       then quickly foreshortened as if I had
            watched it through some distorting
                pane of sun hot glass

          as if by design
              a design of bird
       flat and black
            the birdness removed

from its primordial living and dying circle;
       yet a life is as linear
           as is possible in flight

       where the bird becomes
the flight   star   the direction

       like an object
           against the sky
             NO
       in the sky and not an object
       a mass of lines   defining motion
       and with its motion life

Each life a bird   our sky   day   song and order
      as recorded in each book   of written down life

This summer the sky has dropped its birds
           and doesn't know them anymore

Oranges in January

Enormous
tomorrow
with this unknowing sky   and less air[*]

---

[*] Some 15,000 people died in France during the heat wave of August 2003; several hundred bodies were unclaimed by their next of kin.

Pansy Maurer-Alvarez

PARTICULAR (*for sunrays*)

The foreground races blurred while the horizon
is as still as rock   The clouds
hang there stuck in a painting I think I remember
turning violet in front of my eyes

If the sun were to shine just one day
    again for you
    and for me how lucky   *a little longer*
    we would be in our daisy fields   One spoonful
        for Mommy
        one for Daddy
        for Jack
        and for Grandma but snap
it's the end of January and all gone far away
        somersaulting out
of that yellow light in our daisy daisy fields

        When
        was this particular knowledge going to be given
        to me? To any of us?
        What are they hiding
        in their exquisite box of
        inlaid Japanese lacquer – the lid so loose now
        I can sometimes glimpse inside, and inside
        is where we need to go
        isn't it?

Our seasons stopped one summer
now distance grows in the dark

Oranges in January

I discover my personal compartment
inside the music where the poems go –
where they run with the river alongside me
when night is low, the destination clear.

Pansy Maurer-Alvarez

SPRING'S SUDDEN THIS YEAR AND THINGS CHANGE

Everything I think of is autumnal
Colours seem wrong and the light somewhat startles
the creation of atmosphere and mood   as crows
settling on old branches distort the sunset for me
        from my angle   near the water
                This is eye training for my mind
I imagine countries in the distance   like hills

Try not to bump into anyone standing there
        clumsy so I stumble
and hear: *Carrowmore   Carrowmore*
        now through Neolithic landscapes of
                awakening and wonder   stone after stone

        circumference of stones

Death I'm not interested in
        what I know about it –
                cold and still like a book on a table
But surely our bones
retain a memory of living: of clouds
        of things like jasmine
                or milkweed;
        a foot sliding into a shoe on a
                grey and rainy (again) day;
        of places that were dark and cold, or places
        one should have never been told to leave

For those bodies lying there in ashes   centuries buried
my thoughts   still untitled in my notebook

Oranges in January

return to their stones:
    Strange shining words on water
    words flashing across stone towards the water

Pansy Maurer-Alvarez

COMING AND GOING IN RAIN
for Marcia Mead Lèbre

In a gallery we looked at photographs
              of reflections as seen in street puddles
They could sustain a memory of shadows
       and yellow leaves I thought
the sound of water trickling past us or
                  time we've spent together

Oncoming and swiftly like the swish of wet cars
           the disruption of the water's
optical version of ourselves
      resettles every tiny drop
to collectively form the newly blurred
              outlines of our questions

Because we could not discern their stories
          directly from the photographs
we saw through their images to a place
      that can only be reached in rain when rain
turns us inward for a while
            and slowly shapes a memory

Oranges in January

BARELY HOW THE WIND BLOWS

the shape of former shadows towards me
this night of winter rain in the city

A strong desire for something finite
pushes me to compose
an apology for my middle-age

and reconstruct the image of a younger woman
How her mind almost hurts me to think of it
even as it pricks and challenges the outlines

of the men and women who will define her
No she does not need my protection
although I wish her well this night

in the world someplace gentle –
her dark hair there against the Spanish oranges

Pansy Maurer-Alvarez

PARTICULAR (*for clouds*)

One voice begins
    perhaps shadow   sudden   silver
    perhaps hope
        like another voice a promise
                draws you on and on
you   in particular

Is this what you sense will happen
when warnings
come down mountains thunderclapping
one disguising the next
the sky like slush all winter until you just can't tell
           so
not wanting to but wanting anyway
not holding back
you curl in on yourself
    benevolently
        think: *voices of moon silver   Monday*
        now Venus means rain fragrance and kindness

Still lowered but slowly
                looking a little bit up
you smooth your hand over the page
someplace past the ambivalence of clouds
colours   the whole way from blue to white

Oranges in January

ARCHITECTURE

This room confronts me
slightly darkened by pressure
massively pounding in my chest.
I had thought to eliminate
such dangers and thus
live a simpler
life longer.
But like a model of a never built
funereal monument
the idea stands there
complex and surprising
in its attention to detail
despite the size.
It slows me right down.
This is the first exposition of the red thought.
I can't get close enough with you
in the room.

Red – perhaps a bloodline.
Deeper than blood
where the heart beats in the dark I am
absorbed into the idea like an instinct
although I cannot distinguish
between instinct and idea.
Here are upraised hands, Gothic
with knuckles like flying buttresses.
Think of all the air (or is it light?)
a cathedral
was constructed around.
Imagine all the ideas within one mind.

Pansy Maurer-Alvarez

Think of things you've touched
with the tips of your fingers
and the times when you did nothing.

I circle, I weave
I swirl.
I find the actual working models
that took up the challenge
of conquering three-dimensional space.
Models reflecting different world-views
for pavilions at international fairs:
long model avenues of utopian urban dwellings
habitation clusters on stilts
and bubbles for single-person households.
Towers of all kinds
that were and
for various purposes
ever more shall be
symbolically so
desirable.

I am indoors of the idea now
where I wanted to be with you.
Here is a red circular
apartment skyscraper
hollow and flaring out of itself
with windows everywhere.
Are these the kinds of windows
we could live behind?
Would the light
be right for us in our labyrinth
our Greek temple
our new Babylon or bed of spikes?

Oranges in January

It's tough inside the particles of an idea
floating on air like dust and now I've disturbed
its geometry
its intimate space
by asking how much of this
is necessary to pin down.

The disposition of the red thought
has shifted and is no longer red.
I walk back to that first room with its
18th century project that was never built:
a dark model for a cenotaph to Isaac Newton.
In that locale of mortality and shadow
star-shaped apertures in the cupola
were to have let in the daylight.

Pansy Maurer-Alvarez

FIRST AWARENESS OF THE BLUE LINE

Thin stripe of land between water and sky
flatland, lowland, big sky
whose land? your hand?

    Line of water/waterline
    line where land begins (water? sky?)
In landscape painting, first define line between earth and sky
    line where my leg enters the water
    line along which your farewells stretch –
        when you don't leave except yourself within me

Those islands in the bay seem arranged according
to the rules of chance and you with me here haphazardly
    but we know this isn't so
    We know the light will change
        but not what it will do to us

Oranges in January

PARTICULAR (*for snow*)
i.m. Lucien Fleury

I reach down with my mind to dig up bright petals
                         buried two years now in the snow –
the hall was already full when we arrived so we stood outside in the
       sub-zero evening with others gathered to listen
over loudspeakers to the many tributes with our silent communal heart.
Do we choose the word pain or shock
               over sadness and loss?
Afterwards these places are supposed to become ordinary again.
                 Then how do we clear our throats?

Now I stand at my window estranged by warmth
and watch the obliterating intimacy of snow on the forest floor.
      What in myself
          am I to bring to the present winter's room:
this white landscape without definable source of light
this seeping through of melted snow with its completely
incomprehensible language in a rhythm
              outside my heartbeat?
Everything in nature is particular and nothing gets left out
       but each time, we think nothing has prepared us for this.

Pansy Maurer-Alvarez

THINGS ON THE FLOOR

Insurmountable things on the floor
like black pyramids
which the opera singers
have to skirt, singing.
My mind switches
to those large iridescent
art objects we saw
up tilted on the floor
of a small-town museum
when the large things
on our own floor were
white, rectangular and calm.
But why should I describe them –
we know why they're here.
We're familiar with our things.

Things everywhere on the floor
boxes of things and plastic bags
and things we can't remember

Seed pods
blow in through the window.
Flakes of skin
from our having been here
mix with the dust
our hairs, on the floor.
The only meaning necessary
is this swift organic
movement in our dreams –
this mysterious

Oranges in January

crystalline sadness
in which we appear to lose
our illusions. Awake
we regain our need
to trust benevolence:
Benedictus qui venit qui venit
vulnerable down the path
to look us straight in the eye.
We spend a lot of time
adapting to each other.

Things to get around, things to not touch
Things like dust that disturb an idea
we aren't equipped to grasp

Air rushes across the floor
in waves over us. We watch
dancers finish their work
disengage
themselves from their dance.
Stretching the distance
between them they step
individually out of the circles
of light that heated them.
Then everything goes dark
and still, we're breathless
again in our disillusionment.

A gesture of balance
The long silent page
Some small things remain

Pansy Maurer-Alvarez

WATER-MEADOW WITH BIRCHES
reflections upon the sculpture *Forêt humaine en bronze*, by Ossip Zadkine, 1919;
and the video installation *Effroi* by Natacha Nisic, 2005.

A serene world the forest is so gentle
The water reflects the sky and looks gentle
           Everything is blue
              and green
The wind moves the trees and makes a music I could be seduced by

Watching a video of the water I see a figure
                    walking along the edge of the reservoir
that served the kitchens and latrines of Birkenau
The surface of this water is now moved only by the wind
                        occasionally a frog

Arms like dead branches and birds flying
              we huddle and hold each other together alert
beneath this sky now as though it were water
            reflecting the shadows we know are there –
our nightmare shadows across windows and wall

          Living
          memory

But life
      goes on and people live nearby
Not everything comes to the surface of the water
            Not everything is said or stops

Oranges in January

WORDS CUT UP AND PASTED IN THE MARGINS

Will this glue melt or harden in the sun? Will it
make the pages curl? Will questions come easily
or will they disappear into the air beneath these trees?
Do you read captions carefully enough? Either we know
too much or not enough. It's not always scientific.
But don't believe it. We usually wonder. Do you really
examine the photos? It's happening all around/how close
we are/so why are we outside? We must wait until we're told. When
we're told we can see it. Do you read captions carefully enough? Do
you really look at the pictures? In the middle of
an inaccurate translation, where is the face value? Have we not
been paying attention? These words have been cut off.
And those words have been cut up, however artistically,
into such fine strips, their wispy designs refuse definition.
The cut out words accumulate. They take up too much space.
The growing heap is being swept away from our dwellings.
Have you heard this? Did you see it coming? Have we been
waiting patiently in line all this time? For this? But this
is only the abbreviated version, a caption beneath our photo.
Privately, discreetly, maybe the wind will dispose of it.

Pansy Maurer-Alvarez

VALEDICTION
for my father

Light seems now lighter because your absence
is lengthening.
Sunlight is no longer weighted
with daytime colours and it lifts up almost easily
away from the mountains.
This is absence:
light lingering along the ridges
of the lower hills but gone completely
from the cup-like dips of these familiar Swiss valleys.

When the sun reaches the American continent
it will pass across the knuckles of your beautiful hands
with this same precision.
From between your fingers the light
will leave your grasp and follow its trajectory
into night – where the subconscious memory darts
where dreams are as darkly coloured as water at night
as secretive and illusive
but still reflecting all the light there is.

Oranges in January

DEED

a large shadow appears from left

be it shade
 or somber
  to my thoughts

it is a deed
 if barely
  a cloud

Pansy Maurer-Alvarez

"WITHOUT NOISE OR SPECTACLE"
Barbara Guest

    Starting with pigment
        with a pinpoint
            a second

    with spine
        and skeleton

    composition of skin
        sweat droplet
            disarrangement of light

    My gesture of tossing
    something away
    from its silhouette, its memory of

    Starting anew
        with eyesight
            within earshot and reach

Oranges in January

THE GLIMMERING LONG WINDOWS OF AN AFTERTHOUGHT

How these rectangles of summer light
can stretch and expand
to take hold of a day that was green
gold and soft but now turns somber
as I stand here looking out.
How quickly a single mention
in a magazine somewhere
of *a room with a table and a chair*
guides my thoughts
(when I know I was
thinking otherwise)
back to an old pink room.

Peculiar and dangerous like primeval landscapes
this room of unspectacular things you may think
a room with a table and a chair
by the window. I cannot capture
all the moods or moments contained there,
but behind the eyes
everything
matters in such a still place.
Shall I step back from its threshold
or step into
its light?

It comes,
a chance glimpse
a single mention
it comes across the ocean
comes through windows and it

Pansy Maurer-Alvarez

lies along the lines of an afterthought
then it comes boldly
not hesitating now rushing
this persistence of the room.
Let it come to me
and over me –
I see it in sun
and in silence

see the shiny brown desk surface
of fake wood, the pale gauzy curtains blowing.
I sense a spicy fragrance
of new words like: seraphim
trigonometry, bacchanal or
baccalaureate.
I feel the hard cover of my grandmother's
COMPLETE WORKS OF WILLIAM SHAKESPEARE
digging into my lap for hours, its pages
of India paper as thin
as the dictionary's, the Bible's.
Is there enough light
to read all that
in the niche behind the door
one summer?
This could be happening again and again
in a long row of rooms
with *a table and a chair*
by the window
books and books
and a pen.

A room starts being a room
with its perimeters: floor

Oranges in January

walls ceiling
door windows its yours
when you mark its space or
when it has been assigned
to you and then you do your best.
You mark it with your
thoughts
emotions
and your time.
You protect it from exposure as
it protects you
and you can step into it and back away
from it simultaneously
with a gesture of withholding, of conceding.

I take my room in my hand
to examine its uninhabited time of day
with all its finery laid out in unsuspecting grace:
a desk with a chair by the window
between a piano and a bed.
My bed appears in a painting
on the opposite wall –
a self portrait of a young woman
in a blue dress
sitting on a brightly coloured quilt
on this same bed a generation earlier.
Lying on the bed
I used to pick at the wall until
the white showed through and there was an ugly gouge.
It's chalky to the touch and I keep on
touching it and touching it
and it crumbles.

Pansy Maurer-Alvarez

WISDOM, THE IMMIGRANT, EARTH

To go stepwise
and step sideways, brushing the door-frames of houses being vacated,
a leather jacket over one shoulder making slight noise with each step. Someone
throws open a window
and this part becomes really easy to remember because everything
is in its place, as if it had been committed to recorded memory,
or so it seemed, as it once was, while we stood there catching our breaths
and taking in the full presence of each other again in a room.

I see myself waiting before the mirror of a night retrospectively
where we become shadow play figures recalling drunken party kisses
with reluctance, the new green of leaves down our street in lamplight and blood
one night on your forehead. We are so acute in blame. We come apart
the way trills in the right hand of a high octave lift off the keyboard –
how we feel this in fingers and forearms on certain days more grievously,
more graciously than others. To suppose to know,
to think again.
About such knowing and such desire.

We come striding
out of a thought although it still idles in the room like vapour. To open up
space, to lean into the freed-up space and tend towards each other like this.
To question
durability. We step grammatically into foreign sentences
and as we advance in our phrasing, each syllable
becomes a heavy sentence to be born forthwith out of this shared memory
apprehensively, gravely, and with ceremony.

Oranges in January

To address space tantalisingly, to use figures of speech, because the body
is so important it undulates through our serenity like a beautiful, fragile dress.
Alone, face to face,
without premonition or pretext, we spy through the keyholes
of each other's individualities. What chimera
imposes itself on the sensuality of our imaginings in these moments?

We were pulled into that room,
two people resilient and resplendent, and simultaneously we entered
each other's consciousnesses and foreignness. We weren't looking for anything
we kept saying, we hadn't defined anything yet. Much later we saw
a dark-eyed woman in a painting, clutching oranges to her bare breasts
and staring into the distance behind us; *Naranjas y limones*
that's her space, but sometimes thigh to thigh we ourselves have thought like that,
dipping in and out of each other's vocabularies all afternoon
towards just such a distance. We came to a point
where everything about us seemed curious and we tried to answer for it.

As though another figure appeared in the room to hand us an envelope and the
opening
of the envelope were accentuated by our not expecting
photos of you. Immediately
we fall down the stairwell of the ordinary dimensions of a childhood,
without sentimentality because we think they are diminutive strangers
looking back at us and we might even laugh. To recognise the shape
of a knee, a stance or facial expression that might denote just what holds your
story together. If we veer towards that harmful place, you'll put the photos away
and the symmetrical arrangement depicted before us will be rent asunder, it will
swing up, float and be scattered in the spring air like tree pollen.
To open interpretation.

Pansy Maurer-Alvarez

Small things flower
in the mind and take the shape of a flower opening towards full blossom.
To deposit this flower, respectfully and without any regret for its beauty,
on the windowsill and turn away from the wide open window
in a slow-motion sweep. To look back
at you, to look back on you with a different woman's regard.
Without words in our sonorous throats, without our beautiful arms responding
to the sensuous pull of a departure.

Oranges in January

THE BEAUTIFUL SPELLING OF COMMON WORDS LIKE "PARANOIA" AND "CAMOUFLAGE"

start each morning with
the naming of things around you
as you sense them through dream.
thought is flanked by parched
skull fragments and fumes
from a racetrack photomontage –
the undergrowth is not on fire
but that red behind the eye
is back again, frightening
and blinking again and waiting
for your reaction.
the morning's words stop.
dream is so full of want
you must stay and participate.

Pansy Maurer-Alvarez

ARCHAEOLOGY OF THE LIVING COMPONENT,
THESE SYLLABLES
a sonnet for Alice Notley

Brokenhearted, clairvoyant and shrill, the old dream with the watchful eyes
now appears raw and ungrammatical. The rain is dream, the ache is real.
I can't stop to analyse the spoken word here, I'm hurrying down the street
with my words still fragile, shiny and wet. In the dream I bend over a blue
armchair, I descend the métro steps at Poissonnière, and each moment a new
thought opens into its own sounds. Without imposing boundaries on
coherency, I let these acoustic relations fill my dailiness and you could record
them if you wanted to make them scientific and lasting.

I keep returning to
the place of the poems, despite unrelenting loss of the mother tongue. I don't
believe those CNN accents anymore. My language of grammar and other
memories is not that childhood sound I hear if my brother phones. That's not
the way I'd say it. According to the American publisher, I can't be described.

At la Place de Barcelone, Christian's Swiss German dialect mixes with my
American English: his emphatic consonants, my long ropes of Rs, the dark Ls.

Oranges in January

"CLUTTERED CRYSTAL"
Alice Notley

Every man in Canterbury cathedral
rebuilt a sequence theme for a room

ca. 1410: "Virgin in a Garden"
Master of the Middle Rhineland

Women placed in their silent settings
while thinking about the birth giving

1431: Jeanne d'Arc burned at the stake
1446-50: Gutenberg invents

Swiftly sophisticated in a technical sense
the social silence of failing

1453: Fall of Constantinople
       (to the Turks)

Somebody else who jumps in with something
and takes the subject away from where you were

1471 – birth of Albrecht Dürer
artists and viewers place a gaze within

Forest of ambiguous universe
untamed nature and fabulous animals

24 March 1599: Hexenverbrennung
Margaretha Mössmerin
Catharina Stadellmenin
Anna Wolffartin
beheaded and burned
Freiburg honours memory
suffering   innocent   tortured   atrocities

Written this day in Paris: 1 June 2009
from my notebook by my own hand

Oranges in January

TWIGS, BUNCHES AND TANGLES

Twigs
bunches of
tangled

I thought for a while there was no
    (more) listening
no crackling or time
for acts of listening

Dusty
the leaves
cling to/curl into
arabesques of sorrowfulness
in autumn
sliverlike in sun
they appear
tamed,
doglike

I am awed
    by your manner of addressing, in times like these
    and by some of the motives in artwork

Relics and things
we
    handle, we commerce in, while the forest
        is wide open, is on fire with hisses:
                pine
                fir
                and other

Pansy Maurer-Alvarez

even if you take the fire escape, you don't
    really

We have our whims, we glow and gloss
but we are lacking in *materpieces*

*   *   *

This thing we do
this fine place of first allowance,
(in itself one of my favourites)
        this girth of our maternity waiting
        for more space to clear up in the notebook:
                irresistible forces
                transcended forms
                myth (another favourite)
                dream
                the staggering mistakes and
                foreshortening of our maturity –
        in a sense our fight against
        our own hopelessness
        becomes the art

*   *   *

You have snagged me with your branches
My pullover is snagged and sharp with appeal
It threads itself backwards through undergrowth
It is the charred downside of your secret

Oranges in January

(A WINDOW FLEW OPEN)

Waking to the day's early hour
    with a rose glow it prizes me open;
Sore from fitful reverie, lonely I see
    a man's hands brush his windowsill.

With my shutters folded back
    in that outermost way of moving
I feel weak, peculiar, withdrawn
    as I bend to smooth sheet and pillowslip.

Perhaps it never happened accidentally
    that he stood at an angle for me to see
burnished pediments, corrugated iron
    the copper attraction of distant waterfowl

but warily his substance lingers –
    its uncontrollable dazzle of intent.

II

Januaries

Oranges in January

SYMBOLS FROM THE FATHER-LIKE DREAMS

A place in the moon where the dark river of night passed over my sleep
where I was restless and didn't see
the unbearable, unbroken line of our lives
I never thought of the sun so silently before
The sun shows you where you are, but the shining bodies of the stars
are what you desire – that ascending swing of sun again

The sound of incompleteness:
my leaning shoulder   elbow leaning
lying back   breaking the line
of my thoughts almost faster than I can think
        Deity, do you call upon the dancer every night?
Eyes adjusting to naked night shapes
A sense of what began in dream being lifted into day
        by something changing in the light
Imagined shadows   imagined wakefulness
What depths of involuntary memory are superimposed on us!
        Press a cold wet cloth to your swollen eyes

*   *   *

Let me not move against this cold, with teeth chattering each day since
    my father's death, but touch the air with flat palms, like Eastern
    deities, open, to light the sky ahead of me
The cold weather tears at the new knowledge I'm slowly entering and
    bits fall by my feet like lilac petals in a light breeze to shiver smooth
    my grief

Pansy Maurer-Alvarez

More remote than the horizon through branches at dusk, more so than
the headlights of cars circling the park, in the back of my mind I'm
building a resting place
There was a bugler by the tree they told me but didn't take my words or
want the flowers
How does the heart decide the feet's direction within this new
configuration of the childlove?
No ordinary parting touching my cheek; no watery oblivion available
from the ancient Greeks
But shortly afterwards, a letter about snow geese or tundra swans
migrating, mating and raising their young to be strong enough to
migrate; I've enclosed the newspaper clipping, she wrote.
Another winter sky, another clean page the colour of your rose.

* * *

Light now, this light! Because in your absence I'm dizzy.
It feels so different here, everything's intricate
intact and memorable
in this house within the house I've made in my mind
of you.

All night from room to room my thoughts
roam daringly towards my last remembrance of you.
It's winter I'm cold I'm quiet and I listen.
I'm using my hands along bare walls to remember
things I can't find in my house within a house.
Instead two Japanese dolls and my tiny butterfly pin.
Now I'm lost among objects from childhood and I can't find
what I came for anymore.

Oranges in January

There was something definable and wanted once
in our house.
Now the games have stopped within my family
and I'm dazed in this new configuration of the childlove.

*   *   *

at another level
I dreamt your harsh sounds
your final cry
for water
while the stone finger of the angel
was upon your forehead
pinning you there
to keep you   half-curled
in the disguise of sleep

*   *   *

Salty gloom and worn stone breeze
my reach descends
and in my mind
I am acoustic   Waves
break me flat against something cold
I am labyrinthine
become possessive of the space where you
occasionally appear
exhaling in a recess

Pansy Maurer-Alvarez

TANGIBLE

beginning with a thought stranded in snow
and squinting hard against its winter
its loss of life, of familial relationships

to stall
to decline
to negate

a ringing in the ears like that of a tuning fork
spreads over this tangible landscape
and becomes indistinguishable from it
complicating it

to whine
to declaim
or to remain silent

Oranges in January

(THE CURTAINS OPENED)

the curtains opened   there was
a child crying in her playpen
a child perfectly contained in a ring out of nowhere

one day you will feel so profoundly gratified
and she will continue to adore the father

you have taken such trouble
over the impossible borders
that hover between generations

these continents of time   more fragile
than we had expected, this separate darkness

like a deep opening carved
from imagination or memory
and as soft-sounding as the names they give baby girls

(THE DOORS SWING OPEN)

There is a starless winter's evening
inside the heart of the day. My uncertain alarm
is the solidified syrup of amber
washing ashore, all along the dark northern
coastline.
When the doors swing open like the aurora borealis
an opaque veil of recollection
flickers blue and turquoise without a sound
but with a light that gives me permission
to recognise my these objects on the table
as my mother's.
They are extended vowels, heavy
because they bear their whole history.
Here the O is still clay and water but a bit further on,
she's shaped it and fired it and it opens like lips
in wonder, causing language.
Or beginning to. I murmur something,
one syllable.
I murmur "doll," "mule." "Moon."

Oranges in January

IN THE FORECOURT OF FAMILIAR SOUNDS

Whining   wailing   screaming
Welcome be to the messenger of death, who dances across January
his right arm delineating a purple arc
               for me, three times in January –
Beating of wings, o mortals
Come all ye silently with wings
Recoil not, call upon, open
               delicately but swiftly

      Beyond your beloved faces, stretch the arid terrains
that the deceased, and during the night, the sun
must traverse

I take my leave whining and read
"to the west of the Egyptian cities where the sun sets and the desert
begins, separate but within sight of the living, lie the cemeteries."
Isis is my goddess of the west
         She watches over Inpu, who guides my dead

         After the funeral, the dead
remain heads of their beautiful house of eternity
Their coffins lie underground in a hidden room
         behind another room; this room
    is open to the outside
    and has a sacrifice table
         A stone imitation of a real door

Pansy Maurer-Alvarez

marks the ideal connection between the room of the living
     and the room of the dead
The dead travel between the grave room and the antechamber
To pass through the fake door they may
appear in various forms and little statues
can be put in their graves to substitute them   Mother
moulded an amulet of Bes, who watches over the home
and scares off evil with his ugliness
                    She made lion-headed
Sekmet, who heals but also sends illness and war

I sit in a niche of your tabernacle
while intermediaries of uncertain reality
surround me invisibly
               In the forecourt
colossal statues stare into the distance and sit with

             hand on knee
             knee very close to heart

The doors to the shrine inside the temple
     look closed
               but are opened every day of our lives
The temple where heaven and earth touch
      is cut off by a high wall
              but is our only point of contact now
Only the monumental door allows free passage

To maintain memory, without hindrance to rejoin
O threshold of worlds

Oranges in January

CARNATIONS (I)

There's such a brilliance coming off my desire for some carnations for that dark green jar, that the thought of colour itself stings another desire I have: a desire for three-dimensional space within the folds of the reveries I keep hidden most of the time. For a while I think about crimson, for its sound's sake. Then try scarlet. Then get caught up in sumptuousness and those frilled petals of shelter, trustingly. A child's love bleeds out. The reason for this red desire is not decorative or dramatic or just a tease. Here's a pulse that can be taken and measured against any real one on a fever chart; this makes it a desire that can be understood, commonly. It's what you'd expect, innocently.

Pansy Maurer-Alvarez

NIGHTFALL

Oh wondrous night, where is your prow?

          Interior images
seem to escape from a cave near water level
      although I thought
           I saw lunar landscapes a minute ago

Receding voices line the walls like shadowy figurines
      Warm draughts
          stir a faint scent
Jutting rock shapes look like actors in metallic light

A requiem of rain
    murmurs above the breaking of the waves
Is that tragedy in my singing voice? Will there be
      tragedy along this voyage?

Our imaginary forces are so emotionally charged;
      what it means to have once been
a child comes back,
      the life side and the death side

Loneliness
      because the child's hand in the parent's
is an outline barely visible in this portion of night

Oranges in January

A VOYAGE IN YELLOW LIGHT

     Poor visibility   rising from the central plain
I felt as though I was driving through the language
     of a back   hard and dry,
     of departure
          without formal definition
where all the indicators seemed to have gone missing
          and there was no other mode of transportation

I might have stopped, used my binoculars to watch facial shapes
peel away from the memory of that former place
          but I was a little nervous and thought
     they'd only be masks anyway
          so I kept on through the yellow haze

     I'm lonely in my history
          and I'm fully exposed to it now
This is the material world of landscape and mountain
          a green scarf in the wind

I have never seen the desert
          – out, out to be under the stars –
     and shivering but finally aware

               * * *

Where are you taking me?   To your shelter?
          Are you foregoing? I am.
          We are foregoing together.

This shelter looks temporary.
We might run out of things to say.

When it rains, take shelter.
Be Dido and Aeneas.
It's so obvious!
Isn't that the obvious thing to do?

Oranges in January

DRAW ME CLOSER

Time has split the unfinished skin of dream into a false hollow gold
    and you appear unfamiliar to me now with your awkwardly
    whispered syllables.

I listen for your story remembering the voice I know best but it has lost
    its face like one misplaces an earring, stupidly, and thus
    I am distracted from your sounds.

I know you're telling me something important enough to remember.
    You're describing a picture that isn't a picture. You aren't using
    colours. You aren't using words.

Perhaps if a face can be recorded a phrase will pass through it.
    But isn't that a different story?

Pansy Maurer-Alvarez

CARNATIONS (II)

Render, oh render, render me asunder with your scarlet blooms. Startle me awake and wide to be gifted in purposeful ways. Why am I so fascinated by you? This is all I know about, to come to grips profoundly within the drama of family and raw feelings. Do I really want to call you up from within and inherit what is so hard to dislodge? One reason I try to figure these things out, I hear you whispering to me, is so as not to figure myself out. One image after another in this ultimate writing, stems from that dream image, and the message it leaves you to wander through, you devoutest of pilgrims. To say the word love, out loud.

Oranges in January

DECEMBER

In Philadelphia I am sitting curled up, child with ringlets
      in a series of very small photographs
      Fog as seen in memory –
      evanescence,
      and so forth. Thrall.
You have robbed me of something
      taken something of mine, child, woman,
      dune curve, wave-shaped; flux of women wading
                        to feel fascinated by
Each time I sing I hear you shout across rocks
      clotted and love-stained with centuries
      of murmurings. You don't notice
      it is simply not important to you.
You appear in lunatic colours
      stand in papery light and the air is filled like ice
      with the sound of storms toppling trees.

Pansy Maurer-Alvarez

THE OUTER RIM

All night the poems
     mark the space we've covered
          like diamonds across glass.
Blueprints glimmer but would be so dull
if a whisper were all that counted.

When I think where I've been, some places
darken, hands touch
and lamps dim in an old hotel in New York, which was
mostly red, at least inside my memory of it –
this is not a dream but a tarnished lobby I'm still trying to place.
A blond woman was holding a cocktail glass in an island of sound
alone against the wall under a softly fringed lampshade
and I've been attracted to silky fringe on velvet ever since.

Some days we don't pay enough attention:
     there's too much we don't want to look at
but I think we should have understood more, earlier on.
We didn't intend to form a particular circle around ourselves
     but we thought we knew
what we wanted life to be. Some days
I'm back on the front porch still wanting things to be.
     There's always someone
in the family who takes the jibes patiently, and I wonder
if he led the life he wanted, after all.

     A dark banish like a stain
seeps through to me sometimes in the middle of night
     when alphabets are ephemeral.

Oranges in January

Do not go back to the beginning
               and make a promise.
Another moment awakens
and new vocabulary begins to cling to its malleable complexity;
it grows, this time in bright blue, black and orange.

Pansy Maurer-Alvarez

STILL RADIANT, TRANQUIL SPIRIT

White robe, the gleam of snowy range
     its splendour passes slowly on a glorious scale
        those gleams expire
           blank astonishment
           barrier mountains, peak and spire
        relinquishing them slowly

A thousand blended notes, a flock of birds
     their ascent and cause
     uplifted eyes flashed god-like through
the wind unfurled, the listening lit
           the flaunting leaves

Your long absence haunts me like a passion

Oranges in January

PORTRAITS IN THE HOUSE

It started as the merest twist of the self
in night time agitation like a moth at first inspired,
then driven Was my heart moving faster now
within its unearthly spellbound cage?
Another level opened out like antlers, like waves –
dangerous, at any rate

Because it was natural, rigorous and joyful
    to observe the portraits in the house
        all night from room to room

throughout the house unimpeded

My favourite was never a dream, but the sounds
of a big pale blue city

At what angle to the subject

    You are not being held up, you are spidering down

    All the way alongside the road

A woman waits in the forest
facing north with her story
        word by word, the leaves

Pansy Maurer-Alvarez

Through a pattern of pine boughs, a warble
a shrine sobbed and soaking
a skein
dark blue skein of light

Whispered emerald slippers
repulsive and prolonged
imagine
shaping swans of gossamer tissue
when western light
flickers across the pallid sherbet

Migratory birds

Oh ruinous disbelief!

Every night of the voyage another woman appears
washing the floor on hands and knees,
hair caught up in orchid spangles
Those foldable white chairs get in the way

Near to you and nearer, she says, and this
takes me away again perhaps for the last
time to hold your hand; on another level
of the dream, a stone angel on a pillar
reaches out a finger and points to you
on the forehead

Oranges in January

Struck up and transfixed
when hope comes to a nation, the ground
is sacred
we are clockstill

Sentimental comedy of a majestically satin
ball gown falling off one shoulder as the woman
runs after the man:
I just want to talk, will you talk to me?
kisses placed on the kissable shoulder like newborn birds
he ran like vanity, lasciviously
Despair and Abandonment
I don't need this, forget it
I can always talk to myself!

Water down the body
down the back
between breasts
Robe me in red and silver
remarkable searchlight

there was another event somewhere in the house
there were other voices being loud
there were more voices in some places

Pansy Maurer-Alvarez

WHAT WE RESEMBLE

leaving I cried and fell back
           into the same light ("wild with loss")
placing the core of the thought alongside actual things
in a line of delicate blue

something permanent and illicit in the falling leaves, the dust clouds
Orpheus and Eurydice touching in the park, in profile
with a camera;
a body slumped at sundown, the earlobes, fingertips, toe nails
and halo, the things you cannot speak about
touching wrists, heels

about to fall asleep, with colourful dreams
the sound of water on water, a monastery garden;
        passion and grace (inseparable from redemptive powers)
cradling the wounded animal

* * *

a storm passes, collapsing
        indistinguishable from an old thought
do not believe its flowered print, its ornamental pond

the outcome is the occasion:
a fugue of tile floor, wisteria, the failure of a facade
        and a little bridge of mischief

the final episode is inherited and leaves you no reprieve

Oranges in January

BEAUTEOUS ARBOUR

At a certain distance
the body resembles
more precisely
what happened

A calendar differs somewhat
but looking backwards through tears
a shape clapped its form onto invisible things
to the last point of vision and beyond

What matter if the day be dark –
the purple depths, a soundless breath
flowing and fading, hour by hour
Can't you feel it come and go?

At a certain distance the body
resembles this edge
this creek going underground
under the dark sycamore

Green pastoral, we stood together

Pansy Maurer-Alvarez

THE DISTANCE BETWEEN OUR CONTINENTS

Far from the river
winding spatial flowers
let loose   flattening
fill clearings
The archers escape –
creatures torn from the dark

A master verb
another passage into daylight

In this weather I turn my back
there is no comparison –
terms I think might fit this bright day
We have only pieces of word things left
I sense what might have been

Row of lights
or sleeping nearby
the water earth hope of
greedy green
ebb and flow
time along the river

*   *   *

What I wanted to tell you isn't this:
in this weather you can't tell just any story
It has to be golden and roped

Oranges in January

like a fake theatre curtain, ripped
by design and creased
irreparably, in the right places
or you wouldn't like the outcome
It's that kind of story

In this weather you hear noises
the start of heating
and some machines like music
where rhythm
is more important than you'd think
more than words/works
whose poetic titles attract attention

The room with the juxtaposition
challenged the 1920s critics

"I have made a place."
the distance between our continents
pushing back

Flat
dark wet
roads

Entirely topographical lacerations
many variables fake
Some ideas are so strong you can't help
breathing them in
compliant with my mood
ground down to this

The silence of fields under snow seems absolute at first

Pansy Maurer-Alvarez

Venus in her red-rimmed hat
knows all the medieval byways
forest-struck and smiling
she keeps the key
of course, dangling
over your golden tower
your distant golden tower
Vanity, mist, breath of spirit
not so much as the lack of it
laughter
half stepping out
trees all green around the castle
altered by fingerprints
birdsong/songbirds
contagious, storm-impending
Dürer on the other hand
holding a thistle
engaged, self portrait at 22

Why are flowers such a subject?
beauty, Eros and death
(taken directly from nature)
nude all day

I love loopholes
they're so cunning

Irrigation
ferns
a large pink iris
The seasons' motions happen without us

Oranges in January

yet we are not excluded
Sense and desire, and every thought
you've had is there, wrapped in
air, colour, fragrance

Love poems and eroticisms can so sadden
You depart significantly

* * *

Buildings in a single street or
buildings overlooking each other
along the street to corners' sudden eruptions
But time at this speed diffuses and
only takes up its course near a continent

Walls fences bridges – I love them all
but walls intrigue me today
a stone at evening, a path

My song/love is the city tonight, edgy and torn/sleek
I see the young girls come running down steps
I saw them earlier dressing and undressing
their pink plastic dolls
Figures dance
like black flashes/flames against shop lights/fronts

The metaphor of the tree
and the human forest
freely mingle in the vegetation
Constraints of the natural shape of the stone

Pansy Maurer-Alvarez

shapes and lights and words falling
in the forest   persuasive
bronze   green
tint turned to laurel
Exhale

The will to take up the same motif
repeatedly for the love of its sound
and guide the mind elsewhere

Smokestacks

III

A Dream of Deliverance

Oranges in January

WHATEVER YOU WROTE ON MY DRAWING

Your haze is here again asserting velocity
in my fugitive reasonings

Is that a void where your baby should be?
Or is it a misspelling of body
      of bodily harm, the way you used to play
         with my psyche?

I'm writing these letters down your back
      the broken spine of devotion
My lover's back is a lute
      even more than a landscape
whereas you can no longer distinguish
one mistake from another story
      Subcurrents
every position proving a new surface
Remember how I wanted to ask you about subcurrents?

If there were any places to hide
you would have found them by now –
the places by now known
and unknown in forgetfulness
but re-known

You think you can wind me up with a mere
phone call
you can

Pansy Maurer-Alvarez

Crazy full moon
Little mermaid on her rock
Translate me backwards into the stagnant water
    of dismissive desirability
        to be free
Mouth to ear, look at my shoulder
Flow like a stream still unspoken

Having no home   they are absent gods
I find so striking
in dreams when I need to scream and can't

    Look what I mean
    look what I want you to mean to me

A cold summer is a rain washed block
perpendicularly loosening its diamonds
Do you admire the way   to its maximum
the way a girl whizzes by is pleasurable?

It's impossible to put boundaries
on dressing, a room becomes interesting
when things begin to happen:
birdsong, a woman cleaning windows
repair work going on

I like words to be wild   scattering and dwindling
up and down in arpeggios
    or extended in a well-held arabesque
thus determining perimeters
This is not strange but riskily beautiful

Oranges in January

Orange light, red smoke – let's get colourful
let's further notice things
    in the northern wilderness
    the dizzy ocean
    fata morgana
    the last labyrinth
as fully as we should
A room fills with dancers

Motorists resume their journeys
    just like laughter
the simplicity of the arrangement
Summer trips downriver
felt like luxury, a word filled with traps

There's sunlight in your step today
I will write to you
cornflower blue
Blue finite
darkened to a wheel's sweet spinning
A body in positions
instructions
directions
I don't have your red desire
I am brown wearing black
with unsayable lines
I have been drawing for months
Notice the brown leathery leaves of the sycamore
I need black tones to enable me

Enter with me
the sky space with sun going red
eyes closed with red light inside our vision

Pansy Maurer-Alvarez

a child's tunic
a child's grave
ceremonial belongings:
faithless
drained
unbraided red
from the seed
red from the root of the Indian mulberry tree

The centre of interest is ambivalence of form
      from room to room
There aren't any rooms anymore
in my cold fingers
I think of you
becoming dark

Floral wallpaper
the skeletons of small birds
Ice forms a glaze
at the base of my voice

The physiotherapist
enters the thought of a muscle
and moves all day long
within its painful lingering
      pressing and hunting for more

agonising   ongoing
      Hand hewn ambitions
There's no excuse
I'm reasonably sure
      for these ballroom sashes
           in the face of immense loss

Oranges in January

No arduous steps, no fluctuation
in the space of a field
to see the bottom of the night
removed from his view

She hasn't looked into her files carefully
She knows there's a refining process
      going on inside her
I need for her to be free
      of austere medical legends
Everything has marked this skin
      the jade bracelet was remembrance
      the image flesh

In this room you can't see what's missing
      sometimes we don't notice anything
Inwardly we wept a little
outwardly we built a framework
      What does that sound mean anymore?

As fast as dance movements called fluent
we say goodbye on cheekbones
I was in your country
your boundaries
This is not what I wanted to gather
your brokenhearted human needs and desires;
this is not where you wanted to be either
      so nakedly heartfelt
        your deepest plea

      Head of Janus

In the old burned out house
the sad eye closes

Pansy Maurer-Alvarez

ABSENCE: A PASTORAL

What is that sound? Or this difficult and persistent light? I am difficult to manage in the matter of absence: something illuminated and fitted into the mouth, casting the unimaginable. A roughness on the tongue when overheard. Distorted vision noted, unaccustomed eyelid, skull, skull.

The shape of something in pursuit. Rise and fall. Bow and arrow. Patch of darkness in the story where she slips past embryos and chronicles unnoticed. Muscle and gristle, crucible – a strong odour of metal. Abandonment.

Suddenly leaves, the wood is deaf and formless, a near experience. I am continuing the damage in order to accommodate the punishment of, what do they think this is, Paradise? A narrative of scrawls, my mouth is cut. We are raw, on edge in the movement of our limbs.

The lines of our ligaments magnified, a faint shifting and caking, as paint does when exposed to a final spring. Here is a quiet blue flame. It is morning.

Oranges in January

A DREAM OF DELIVERANCE

I have only one sleep
      the envious wait
undressing   delicately faced
I don't know how to approach this kind of wave

The coldest looking part can happen in a forest
blurred beyond the reach of light
Slide over countryside, start a poem
      deeper than blood
Are you famous for hypocrisy?
"The sky had the last word" Fanny Howe

Ice floe –
are you shaped into the *e*
of that word I've liked since grade school?
Point downwards on bright blue

Wail like a dog,
if you can look at it that way, Dubai
I cannot rest you on my knee

This woman is a spoken role, with a mouth on
laughingly
      on sunshine
with the deep rule of wide behaviour
Near daughter attention
moves backwards through interpretation
comforting with my lips   the missing children

Sting and stench of the actual
coming down

Drink the cut cord
drink the spent breath
they look like iron bars
and blood on a pillowcase
I will devour myself with violence and remorse

"the vibration of a peculiar touch" Barbara Guest

Sink back into
incomprehensible countryside

I have one sleep, delicately faced
transgressing and scratchy
Ah, the suffocating gauze

(I like the idea of a patron saint
somehow tiny lights play a role):
       Magnolia
       Questions against the morning
       Soft fire
       Hair falling
       Show me

When they are all finally within myself
watching the distraction of her take place
circling the head
an inclination to head off
and split the particles of his gaze

Oranges in January

endless pattern seeking spring
one voice begins:
edge
upheaval
frost flowers
canopy and banner

veil of foreshadow
shadow sudden river

like an aquatic pleasure, the closer I get to the poem
So many people gather in these public rooms where lovers meet

art in public places
organic shapes
spatial constellations determined by chance
dream paintings
space, line and balance

the black seed

Instead of men, a rather pretty actress
folklore
restless, worn, broken with limp

Out of my window of pale light
deepest point in the lake
dip in the road
Look at the silence and energy in paintings

seems alive but is not life
tries to leave   no space
wants to use full range of voice

Pansy Maurer-Alvarez

Above my head his face high in a light
somewhere in a light outside dimension I thought
I remember various voices struck us the night we met

The professor said that sex
was another way of saying life
and I noticed some women taking notes

Angeltime when angel means
mediator, leaves us when he's done what he can

Memory dreams all mixed up by now
Now I have the ghostly
mis-hearing, through enormous shadow
consequently at moments of sunrise
one-to-one

It's cold from doors open straight onto the street
pigeon feathers

a dream of deliverance

Oranges in January

PICTURE OF FICTITIOUS WATCHMAN WITH HAWKS

A house from the outside, painted   within the limits
     of a personal conversation
     between parents
These window panes are mine now   in reaction

A simple dislocation can look like untruths
There was an anticipation of will power, a strong will of power
     of ownership   overpowering
Torn pieces of   depictions of   in tatters
     I just fall to pieces
The loss concentrated itself on this –
it keeps coming closer with whisperings

I'm drowning
     because I think too much, remembering
that which he has certainly forgotten during the day
but it's inflicting my night space and recurring
Things I didn't want
when their power took me for their purposes
I looked up   like in nature
where certain creatures are always on the scurry

My body is falling down with birdsong
in beautiful lavender notes   the sum of its parts
The chronic angers still look down from such height!
I don't want to   I don't want this

vertigo in the recurring dream where I defend
my poetry with serrated fractures (Oh, my music, my sword!)
to a kind-looking man with blue eyes and curly hair

Pansy Maurer-Alvarez

who likes understanding so much he wants to understand
so he can feel
     just the same way terrible as I
         do
It doesn't matter where I am   he enters a room
     swifter than physical attraction
A little, yes, he's a little sad
       maybe a bit tired
I tip toe away, then suddenly we're face to face
and my fear is more tangible than a sharp pinch

Oranges in January

RESTLESS DEPICTION INCLUDING A WATER ANGEL

I'm in the foreground with a dog and a cat,
  thinking of painkillers and painters in churches

Strange music, so the stirring must occur
  somewhere unawares

Gleam whatsoever golden of rain remaining, for a while
  we are not broken

To the thin edge a child, maybe in wet clay
Everywhere in nature that river light, joylessness
  unnerved you, you didn't say a word
The simple act of reading a letter, turning
  towards the light with head inclined, eyes so ruined
  the writing dances, the wrong person in the dream
  waits at the stage door

Chinese embroidery unravels its own riddle
  higher than the palace, as if we were all
  exploring rooms or nervous systems
The strange feeling when a man puts his hands
  on the level of how it happened –
  you turn into something you remake
  and reside there for a while, effectively denied
Grouping and scattering particles of tones
  alive, restless with blue shade, a parting gift

Your casual way, sticky yellow, down the street
  in your cotton dress

Pansy Maurer-Alvarez

Then he does the beautiful promise thing
   for you in the husband way, binding a thread
   which could be passionate or merely
   securing sequins to your neckline
Someone's always a masquerading love instrument
   and everything sounds poetic this way
Not even his hands could be

Small tables with red chairs
Lots of women chewing lettuces
The fragrance of fruit pies baking while
   "What's in this soup?"
I've been listening to women,
   so much goes into their aspirations:
   jargon, entanglement, portrayal
   arrays, bewilderment
   because love can sometimes be boring
There is evidence that it can be a hot new field
The skin of our language can be memorable music

I found a different tremble, all afternoon
   with a dull dwindling, retreating crumpled
Swallows dipping
   darting upstream
   along the stretch of stubble to the inlet
This coastline is fluttering and intricate:
   leaves in the wind
   a water angel, wader of dreams
Something amazed the light facing me
   rinsing away many years' damage
I was knotted in a place
   where stubborn interfering
   distorted my anticipations like black smoke

Oranges in January

Choking, twitches –
 arms at my sides, incidentally

I'm going to reverse the female garden image
 and take the men with their delicate insteps
 along paths
Go down deeply and plant something kernel-like
 I say to myself, not to them

Let the dim cathedral cool your skin
I barely remember your mindfulness
The conference on language collapsed

Pansy Maurer-Alvarez

FOR THE CENTONARII
4 cento sonnets

I.

Everything in the city comes to this table
dearest ear, l'oreille cassée, nose for my eyes
even before I saw the chambered nautilus
I dreamed of a clipper ship

the place between yr legs which is the place
It's only with clumsy freedom that things appear on people's lips
held together by an almost experimental sonnet
Lavender and heart-shaped

As ladybugs swarm, two guys in a jeep stop for beer
I get up, white coat, glance out at the rain
this is a song about the weather
green air astounded by your passage

What a pleasure it is to undergo the days
Oh wet kisses, the poem upon the page

Oranges in January

II.

Explosions of laughter at the stairhead
and slow time, assent, decline, premier something or other
Other than what's gone on and stupid art
So you fucked me back in
get afternoon dark I do
Can you believe this shit?
So there's hardly need to play on abstract repetitions
Mocking your back-broke beauty
While a painter loads a brush. Profanity recedes
Love in a capsule coated with loss, never
brushes against the consonants
I wanted to mouth you all over

the smaller than usual muse
does not point to William Carlos Williams

Pansy Maurer-Alvarez

III.

Our day began on a dull red door
shadow of my digression, a new vague shape of day, fig
That in my vagina would fall a drop of cock
Being part in part outside the premises
who touches this touches a woman
There goes something forever lost in context
to satisfy a predecessor, poet, lawbreaker: I won't be clever
Humans shouldn't figure. Let alone ...

Nobody likes this poem. It's intelligible, yes,
The bitter cup but true of flesh-driven earth
is brought into the present
the mouth that smiles will speak for itself
drifts past and turns
And the sonnet is not dead

Oranges in January

IV.

We sank in becoming colour poured on
black or blue, like your browning eyes, is a bell obscene
Love's not intent today what did I see
Invisible upstairs in seclusion
I spring into your arms in Whitmanic what
She will never believe she's too old to join a band or make quick
      vertical moves on the playing field to really quiet music – she's
      that still
Once more, almost a joke – this most serious endeavour
So. Tock. Sound. Or light. Partly stone.
Like trees we must wear the flesh all our days
Holding a stranger's thin arm I turn down the light
a colour of equal repose
The lovers in the fountain spoon each other up
Such warm pockets in your belly, your corduroy
Still they mean something. For the dance

    The first line of each cento comes from John Welch, the second from Stephen
Rodefer, the third from Bernadette Mayer, then Alice Notley, Eléni Sikélianos, Lyn
Hejinian, Robert Adamson, Geraldine Monk, Geoffrey Young, Peter Riley, Thomas
A. Clark, Michele Leggott, Ron Padgett and Ted Berrigan.

Pansy Maurer-Alvarez

PERFORMANCE PIECE FOR NOTEBOOKS
from the notebook I numbered 3

barefoot the dream
      would appear to him, would begin without preliminaries
her words rustling mercilessly
         "I doubt you
         I doubt you wholly and truly
         not just when I'm awake and wandering."

before the time of the dream's regular interruptions, the poet
would lie down in the poets' garden and wonder *What kind of
person could cover me completely with the black seed of thought?*

Once hard and stalky, he can now speak only in musty fragments:
         in a previous garden   a relative of
         by the petals and the leaves
         erect   dark and slender
         delectable perennial
         may suffer   will evaporate

I am now further ahead than ever except in my memories of it
         city wet

I went to a party of needs where the women mingled
                  mapping out
available the way I see it now
      I'm saying my stuff
         with their noses in the news

Oranges in January

Wardrobes fill by the way they chose
(passes from woman to woman like a pageant)
his overcoat mattered so much

I have offered and forgotten
        that I have left so many impressions

                this thwarted me
                in the space of absolute silence
I will probably only ever want
one moment at a time   the present
(history is a long list of disputables
                        wanting things)

disputables waylaid at the costume ball
waylaid in public transportation   iridescent and fanciful
careless
and seductively watching the subtle movement across
our wall of erotica and companionship

                Fixing a point to live towards
                        gets refracted
                the balance is not bearable
                when you try to live it:
                performing and dissolving

Pansy Maurer-Alvarez

SEVEN VIDEO CLIPS

I.

traces are not the proof but still I take you
seriously, blue shape
dancers   at the opera   details of
a nude woman, the movement of her scarves.
a small change in the house
heartbeat   daybreak   heartbreak
old   new   repetitive.
she brushed past me in a light strapless dress
she was taking liberties with the space and
the little boat of happiness I carry under
my left arm   a gorgeous slip of paper
barred my path   others were gathered there
in the flowery blue   fluid   light.
you can be fooled and so can I, I remembered
so we turned back and became a duality
once more.
eddy of breathlessness   breastbone
closely explore the texture and shake water
from your hair
without directing a camera, the artist
includes her own body in the process.

Oranges in January

II.

    timorous optical ghost
        criminal windfalls
            common law

    a part of each other
        and others gathered apart from

    here's a scrap of paper

    free will
        brute force
            in favour of
                disobedience

Pansy Maurer-Alvarez

III.

For the loss of a green pool wilderness
      poppies sway while birds fly through a story
                    steady and rising
Symmetrical arrangements of garden furniture come into view
There is no naked joy here, no one blinking and ready to be lost again
Every place where someone is is just a place, a man with a sandwich
A group of actors milling under the trees, while the man who knows them
      places his hand in the middle
          of my back and explains (them to me) softly
      and why could no one see us by the fountain a few feet away?
The things that two people say in private, the desires they give up
I will write these things on my body in lines of minute description
      What surprises me is the silence

Oranges in January

IV.

The birds are low over the marshes reflecting the last thoughts of day
The woman might be ready to go out in her flimsy floral print
The dislocation of her melancholy might allow a glimpse of the landscape
      where her legs and feet appear beautiful but don't matter
Her whole being becomes a nesting ground for birds
No one ever fully explains the sky

Pansy Maurer-Alvarez

V.

A woman lies there in her new cocktail dress at a disjointed angle to herself
her arms and legs at impossible angles
and charcoal delineates the contours of her body from thigh to hip
waist, shoulder, jaw

blurred contours instead of sharp silhouettes
misty   drizzle   rainwater
                                      water-colours

* * *

You're so smooth, he'd said to her, smooth over, move over, soothe me
         in your off the shoulder gown
                  cream-coloured
                           satin,
                           fetching,
                                    in your off the shoulder manner

* * *

A magpie must have swooped down and stolen something
         bright
she wasn't really watching, she was trusting but now
she notices something's gone

Oranges in January

VI.

This interior is an enormous breathless wrap
resembling snow-covered hill tops
and a soaked-through upholstered horizon

foot bridge   hairline in the distance

A voyage that was never really understood
its turbulent dipping frightening
Although I sometimes appear weary
I am agitated and recognisable

Pansy Maurer-Alvarez

VII.

I am set apart, witnessing my tender realm:
a family's outlook can be a blank stare or
an injured look when someone suddenly sits up
and takes notice, deliberately

I'm struck by something that was unapparent in childhood

the small garden house
where rooms grow cold, drip, drip, the water,
the wide kitchen sill lined with
oranges in winter, tomatoes in summer,
but most of all the pink gauzy room
I shared until the day her bed was removed
to make room for the newly purchased piano
no space, no space for her in our house

I appear at the edge of this description
I come to the desk in that room
that room slips back into memory but now
I enter the poem bare in my mind

Oranges in January

POEM

and maybe these poems are just fondling her example
like good manners in a sad family of failures
but my favourite was never a dream
and these things happen anywhere

Pansy Maurer-Alvarez

INTERCHANGEABLE DISTRACTIONS

Here I am in my spring-like mood before you. What are you reading?

"Lily of the Paginated Tundra"

and the blossom-holder is touched by the smell of rain.

I picture myself received in nearness impossible to describe.

But why are you crying in little parts, breaking up into crystals?

I don't want you so handsome anymore, leaning forward in that gesture
just before leaving

Am I blocking out my alien angels again?

There's no peace or relief in these rooms, small overnight bag of notebooks –

take a look around you.

There was something definable and desired in the shape of our outlooks.

Sunlight falls across me now, it doesn't slant.

I will step aside for you.

I will attach substance to your matter.

The things I'm prepared to do for unkind people, parachutes and lilac
are more poetic.

Oranges in January

WHEN YOU THINK YOU'VE NEARED THE END OF THE STORY

(why have these) paisleys become traits in your throat
that reservoir of snails   so mad and muddy you can
coax/hoax your way through it when
the shapes of bodies scraping and nudging
come at you rustling to singe your prayers

Paradise is everything in its place
We're having a meaningful relationship here, so just let us be
I haven't been here long, not half long enough
It's not just the bed that's unmade, there's always more going on in the
original (room)

Pansy Maurer-Alvarez

INTERIM

this parting   vibrates   with the speed
        of things magnified   measuring
        a curious detail

    pearl and opal are adequate intervals
balancing the pale iris swell, overspilling moods
    ruptured   and things to try: musical
instruments   tuned   like footsteps intervening
        across flagstones

    under wet tone arbors   we'll find our measure
who touches the dark maiden afternoon grows pale and turns around
    I wanted you all afternoon
    I wanted you all over
    and over   again

Oranges in January

SCATTERED BEADS

the scattered seed pearls, beads of cancer, someone's Pap Smear, MRI, breast cancer, popsicle man ice cream van, there's no little ice cream man inside your breast, your intestines, your heart brain.   there's no treacle tart test with double cream for you.   take this bread and wine, of body and holy blood, the Christ who bled for us, turn to his body whole, I have taken Communion but I have never communed.   the sounds that rise from the smudge on the floor, floorboards staging a scene to be played out on the disinfected linoleum tiles of OP rooms, people without their sounds waiting for it to happen.   the brevity of the throat, the poem.   life-threatening life-enhancing life-lengthening. the bedside shrine is saint-like with orchids, a glass of water, visitors to stay 5 minutes only, they want to hear the story but can't deal with the outcome, who can, what do we say, what does the outcome come out of? skin hair chaos betrayal, your little body's cathedral is prone, are you at peace, asleep or in contempt of?   in need, we are in need, needy, needlessly craving for, we haven't found the grace yet, the grandeur the lesser to be with, we are burning our little picturesque performances as we go for fear, we are so afraid, the darker we go the nearer we get. and we still don't know how to answer.   the splinter, the components, piecemeal, temporal, mosaics shattered, scattered beads from torn necklines, confined to, we are confined to our rooms for fear – this is the texture of our faithlessness, our greedy swollen golden filaments.   we don't answer the doorbell, we want to know who's on the line before we answer the phone, our dreams twisting round the moon the stars, our majestic real life, our single-minded wrath when it grows cold, cold grows on a stem and its flower is bluish white.   tramp on to an unknown destination with bells and drums and a gong, cup your hands around, clap your hands, hands offering a piece of,   I have come from afar you say, I have come so far for you, how far can you go, you ask will you?

Pansy Maurer-Alvarez

what wave of love of broken-hearted weariness, honeysuckle by the wayside, crucial memory of beauty that lingers between fingers fingering the bed linens, hair skin and chaos from before recounted memory, when we were once so newborn and that endangered.

Oranges in January

SOME ROOMS WERE FICTIONALLY RED

Why are they closing the doors to the rooms? It is the abandoned space, the enclosed room all by itself now that I lament. Clack. Slam.

You're going to catch cold in that open space with a windy hilltop despite lovely view of the imaginary line where we met. Come back.

First night together. In a room. Multiple rooms for multiple selves. Different languages and lights burn inside them. Elsewhere, perimeters.

Excavated villas. Segment of wall with traces of pigment: yellow bird on branch.

A resounding series of scenes, my *angoisse*: surrealism in a stance on the patio as seen through the window; kaleidoscopic solitude, darkened and dream-scarred. Then someone says *Industrial Landscape with Stork and Pear Tree* could be a good title for a depiction.

WE FIT IN A ROOM

We fit in a room, a quiet room, and in a minute, shiver
cradling the old question sadly diminished in stillness
This makes me curious and eager for meaning
Is this the natural feeling after all these years?

Not prepared to   does not mean
unprepared   from a distance resembling a smoke wreath
The Sirens have drowned the sound of rupture and the morning
offers its gathering of animated shapes against another light
A natural feeling starting to come apart, becomes basic
that we might have already come to the final room

And if I bring to the table what I have found
the error of what I have found
and put it all into words
not necessarily harsh but lengthy, distorted, would you be
concerned, or if not concerned, curious?

Your left eye, profile, ear, the sheen on your skin from
    my angle beside you
We've come to our table now unable to speak
for fear of becoming unreal and separated
A grey memory of waiting in a Belgian lobby
watching passersby through a vine-darkened window
They could be anyone going anywhere
Everyone here is going someplace
I thought then not knowing

Oranges in January

We live among our things, pressed next to people
knowledgeable with questions
and this is the way some stories are told –
to imagine ourselves, others   what facts there are
"This is our jubilation
Exalted and as old as that truthfulness
Which illumines speech."
A good cook   her cheek, her mouth and kitchen scales
beyond the rim of her plates   light-headed
distinctly dislocated, unruly yet sufficient
"It is not the wild glare
Of the world even that one dies in."
What was it, that single thing I wanted more than anything?*

---

*   Quotations from "Of Being Numerous" by George Oppen